Weekly Reader Books presents

Heroes of the Civil War

Abraham Lincoln

By Susan Dye Lee

Illustrated by Ralph Canaday

 CHILDRENS PRESS, CHICAGO

This book is a presentation of Weekly Reader Books.
Weekly Reader Books offers book clubs for children from
preschool to young adulthood.

For further information write to:
Weekly Reader Books
1250 Fairwood Ave.
Columbus, Ohio 43216

Library of Congress Cataloging in Publication Data

Lee, Susan.
   Abraham Lincoln.

   (Heroes of the Civil War)
   SUMMARY: A brief biography of Abraham Lincoln
who was President during the Civil War.
   1. Lincoln, Abraham, Pres. U. S., 1809-1865—
Juvenile literature. 2. Presidents—United States
—Biography—Juvenile literature. 3. United States
—History—Civil War, 1861-1865—Juvenile literature.
[1. Lincoln, Abraham, Pres. U. S., 1809-1865.
2. Presidents] I. Canaday, Ralph. II. Title.
III. Series.
E457.905.L4   973.7'092'4   [B]   77-20125
ISBN 0-516-04701-9

In 1861, a Civil War broke out between the North and South. Men on both sides joined the fight. Most of them had never been soldiers before. Some were not much older than you.

Early during the war, one young soldier—a northern farm boy—got into trouble. He fell asleep while guarding his post. For this mistake he was put on trial and sentenced to death. Only the President of the United States could save him.

Now the president knew army rules. The North could not win the war with sleepy soldiers. But in this case, he signed a pardon for the young man. He did not think the boy deserved to die.

Several years later, this same farm boy died in battle. In his pocket, fellow soldiers found a picture of the man who had once saved his life. Across the photo he had written, "God Bless President Lincoln."

People remember Abraham Lincoln for his stand against slavery. People admire Abraham Lincoln for his leadership during the Civil War. But people *love* Abraham Lincoln for his goodness and mercy towards others.

Abraham Lincoln came from country roots. He was born in 1809, on a log-cabin farm in the backwoods of Kentucky. It was a cold winter day, the twelfth of February.

The baby's parents named their first son Abraham, after a grandfather who had been killed by Indians. Abraham was the second child of Nancy and Thomas Lincoln. He had a sister Sarah, age two.

The Lincolns were plain folk. Abe's father was a farmer. He grew corn, hay, and other crops. Abe's mother helped him.

The Lincolns farmed the land without slaves. In 1809 slavery was still legal in the southern states of our nation. Kentucky was a slave state. But Abe's parents did not believe in owning slaves.

Little Abe grew into a strong boy. He helped his father plant seeds. He hoed the garden and pulled weeds. He carried water and wood. He kept the fireplace clean. There was always another job to do on the farm.

During the winter months, Abe and Sarah went
to school. The rest of the time, they had to work on
the farm. In those days, the law did not make
children go to school.

Abe began learning his A, B, C's when he was
five. He liked to write. He wrote letters in the dirt,
in sand, and in snow. Words interested him.

In 1816, the Lincolns moved to Indiana. They
reached their new land in December. Seven-year-
old Abe could not believe his eyes. Huge trees

covered the land. The forest was full of bears, wolves, and other dangerous animals. It was a wild, raw country.

For a few weeks, the family lived in a three-sided shed, called a lean-to. On the open side, a fire burned day and night. It kept them warm and frightened animals away.

During this winter, Abe learned to use an ax. He chopped wood for the fire. He helped clear the land for spring planting. He split logs for fences.

9

Abe also helped his father cut logs for the new cabin. The floor was only dirt. But it had a loft, where Abe slept.

One day in the cabin, Abe heard the beating of wings. He grabbed his rifle, aimed it through a crack, and shot a wild turkey. But Abe was not proud of himself. He did not like killing, even for food.

Bad luck soon struck the Lincoln household. In 1818, Abe's mother got the "milk sick" and died. Without her help, the family could barely keep going.

The next year, Tom Lincoln went back to
Kentucky to find a wife. His children needed a
mother. In December, he married Sarah Johnston,
a widow with three children. Now seven people
lived in the one-room cabin.

Abe liked his stepmother. She cared for him. Like many frontier women, she had not gone to school. But she wanted Abe to get an education.

Abe was a curious boy. His mind was open to new ideas. He listened. He looked. He asked a lot of questions. He thought.

Abe learned from books, too. He read the *Bible* and *Aesop's Fables.* He read about George Washington. The lives of good men gave him ideas. He began dreaming dreams.

Tom Lincoln did not understand his son. Abe read in the fields. He read during meals. He read by firelight. Why did he always have his nose in a book?

"What I want to know is in books," Abe said. "My best friend is the man who'll git me a book I ain't read."

In truth, Abe looked more like a pioneer than a bookworm. At 16, he stood well over six feet, with legs like stilts. Chopping had given him strong arms.

For the next few years, Abe worked as a hired hand. Neighbors paid him 25¢ a day. By law and custom, he gave this money to his father.

But Thomas Lincoln was still unhappy. Crops were poor. Stories of better land in the west made him restless. In 1830, the Lincolns moved to Illinois.

During his first year in Illinois, Abe did a lot of thinking. He did not like farming. Surely life had more to offer. But what did he want? It was time to find out.

And so, at 22, Abe left home. He moved to New Salem, a log-cabin village on the Sangamon River. For the next few years, Abe took all kinds of jobs—store clerk, surveyor, and mill hand.

Abe joined the war against the Indian Black Hawk. He became a captain. But he and his men never fought any Indians. "I had a good many bloody struggles with the mosquitoes," he later joked.

In 1833, Abe Lincoln became the postmaster of New Salem. Abe liked this job.

Abe was soon well-known by his neighbors. They liked the tall young man who read everything and carried letters in his hat. They listened to him talk about the news of the day. They liked his ideas and trusted his honest ways.

Politics and government interested Abe. In 1834, he ran for office and won. The people of his county elected him to the Illinois legislature. The legislature made laws for the people of the state.

During this time, Abe decided to study law. All together, he had spent only one year in school. So he had to study hard. He taught himself by reading law books.

In 1836, Abraham Lincoln passed his law
exams. The next year, Lincoln opened a law
office in Springfield, the new state capital. Lawyer
Lincoln won many cases. He understood the law
well. He was very clever, too.

In one case, a rich man asked Abe to get $2.50 owed to him by a poor man. Abe took the case for $10. Then he went to the poor man and gave him $5. The poor man then paid the rich man and had $2.50 left over. The rich man was happy, and Lincoln made $5.

Lincoln may have been bold in front of a jury. But he was very shy around women. His looks were homely, and his suits never fit. He didn't know how to make small talk.

Then Abe Lincoln met Mary Ann Todd. He liked her quick, outspoken manner. But the thought of marriage gave Lincoln cold feet. At last, he proposed. Mary Todd and Abraham Lincoln were married on November 4, 1842.

The Lincolns found many joys in their new life together. They became parents. In time, they had four sons.

The next few years were busy ones for Abraham Lincoln. In 1846, he ran for the United States Congress and won. As a member of Congress, he spoke against slavery. He did not want new lands in the west to become slave states.

During the 1850's, differences over slavery began to divide the nation. In the North, the book, *Uncle Tom's Cabin* told of the evils of slavery. More and more northerners began to say slavery was wrong. They wanted any new states joining the Union to be free. They did not want slavery to move westward.

Southern whites did not like this. Most of them believed slavery was right. They wanted new lands in the west to become slave states.

In 1856, Lincoln joined the Republican Party. Most Republicans disliked slavery. Lincoln talked against slavery. He often asked slave owners this question. If slavery was a good thing, why had he never heard of a free man who *wanted* to be a slave?

Soon, Lincoln became an important Illinois Republican. In 1858, the party picked him to run for the United States Senate against Stephen Douglas. Douglas was a leader in the Democratic Party.

Before the election, Lincoln and Douglas held many public speeches. They argued about the westward spread of slavery. Lincoln wanted new states joining the Union to be free. Douglas did not care, one way or another.

On election day, Douglas won the Senate seat.
But Lincoln was not really a loser. His speeches
with Douglas had been published in newspapers
all over the country. People began to talk about this
western lawyer who said: "I think slavery is wrong,
morally and politically."

Two years later, in 1860, Republicans met in
Chicago, Illinois. The meeting was held to pick a
man to run for President of the United States.
They chose Abraham Lincoln.

Once again, Lincoln ran against Douglas. This time, Lincoln won. All the states in the North but one went for Lincoln. In the South, he got only a handful of votes.

Many southern whites were upset at the election of Lincoln. They did not want a president who said slavery was wrong. The slave-holders were worried. They feared Lincoln would set their slaves free.

After Lincoln's election, seven southern states left the Union. They did not want to be part of the United States any longer. In 1861, they formed a new government. It was called the Confederate States of America.

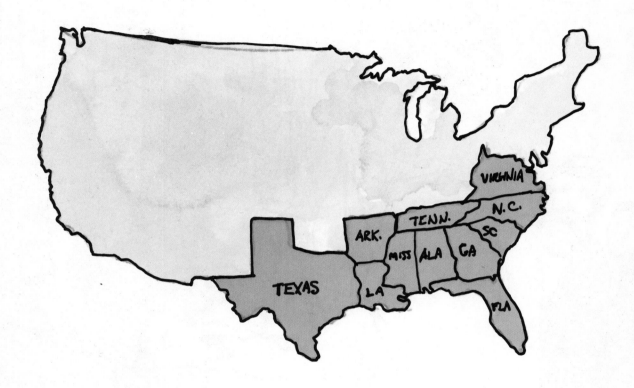

Would the United States let the southern states leave the Union without a Civil War? The whole nation was uneasy. No one knew what was going to happen.

On March 4, 1861, Abraham Lincoln took
office as the sixteenth president. A large crowd
heard his speech. The president told southerners:
"We are not enemies, but friends."

But Lincoln's words could not mend the differences between North and South. The North and South went to war. The fighting began April 12, 1861, at Fort Sumter, South Carolina. News of the fighting spread quickly. Men on both sides signed up for army duty. Both sides counted on a short war.

For the first two years the war went against the North. Union armies fought well, but they needed better leaders. President Lincoln tried one general after another. None of them could beat the Confederate general, Robert E. Lee.

President Lincoln soon learned how to run a war-time government. Men had to be drafted into the army. Soldiers needed guns, clothing, and food. Railroads were needed to move men and supplies. Ships were needed to block southern ports. The president spent a lot of time on these problems. He was always busy.

People came to the White House every day asking for favors. A long line always stood outside the president's door. He wrote hundreds of pardons for soldiers like the farm boy. He even found people jobs.

On January 1, 1863, President Lincoln signed the Emancipation Proclamation. This act freed many slaves. However, it did *not* end slavery completely. Some black people still remained slaves.

"If my name ever goes into history," Lincoln said, "it will be for this act, and my whole soul is in it."

The Emancipation Proclamation freed slaves in most of the Confederate States. As a result, thousands of black men joined the Union army. Many white soldiers were unhappy about this. But President Lincoln would not change his mind. "I am a slow walker," he said, "but I never walk back."

In June of 1863, General Lee marched his army into Pennsylvania. At Gettysburg, Lee's army met Union forces. For three days, the two armies fought. This was one of the bloodiest battles of the Civil War. On both sides, a total of 7,000 men died.

When it was all over, the Union army had won.
On July 4, Lee began moving back to Virginia.
The defeat at Gettysburg was a terrible blow to
Confederate hopes.

In November the battlefield at Gettysburg
became a National Cemetery. President Lincoln

went there to honor the war dead. A large crowd listened to him say: " . . . we here highly resolve that these dead shall not have died in vain—that this nation, under God, shall have a new birth of freedom—and that government of the people, by the people, for the people, shall not perish from the earth."

In 1864, President Lincoln found a winning general. He put Ulysses S. Grant in charge of all the Union armies. During that year, northern armies began to crush the life out of the Confederate States.

President Lincoln hated the loss of life on both sides. As a boy, he had disliked shooting a turkey. Now, the human bloodshed made him sad.

In November of 1864, Abraham Lincoln was elected to a second term as president. By now, it was clear that the war would end soon. Already, the president had plans for the South. He wanted the southern states to re-enter the Union quickly and easily. He had no wish to get even with the South.

On March 4, 1865, Abraham Lincoln was again sworn into office. Thousands heard Lincoln speak of his hopes for the future:

"With malice toward none; with charity for all; . . . let us . . . do all which may achieve and cherish a just and a lasting peace, among ourselves, and with all nations."

One month later, on April 9, 1865, General Lee surrendered to General Grant. Lincoln was overjoyed. Soon the United States would be whole again.

The next day, Washington went wild with joy. Guns were fired, bells rang, and bands played. A crowd in front of the White House called for the president. Everyone cheered when he came outside.

The evening of April 14, the Lincolns went to see a play at Ford's Theatre. They came late and sat in the President's Box. The audience cheered Lincoln's arrival. Then the play continued. The president laughed and began to relax.

Behind Lincoln, a door opened softly. No one saw the man in a black felt hat and riding boots. It was the actor, John Wilkes Booth.

Quickly Booth slipped inside. Then he stepped forward, pointed a gun at the president's head, and fired. The president fell forward in his chair. Mrs. Lincoln screamed in terror. People panicked.

The president was carried to a house across the
street. Doctors came. They shook their heads.
There was no hope.

All night long the president fought for life.
Hours went by. A hard rain began to fall. Down in
the street, people stood waiting and praying. But it
was no use. At 7:22 on the morning of April 15,
Abraham Lincoln died.

News of the president's death shocked the
nation. In the streets, in the churches, and in
homes across the land, people wept. They sought

comfort in words. They talked of Abraham
Lincoln's belief in justice and fair play. They
praised his kindness, mercy, and understanding.
Many felt like they had lost a good friend.

The president's body was placed on board a train
for Springfield. Thousands lined the route. At
every city, town, and crossroad, people stood in
silent sadness. At night, their torches and bonfires
lit the sky. Finally, the train rolled across the
prairies into Illinois. Abraham Lincoln had come
home for the last time.

IMPORTANT DATES

1809	February 12, Abraham Lincoln is born in Hardin (now Larue) County, Kentucky.
1816	Lincoln family moves to Indiana.
1818	In October, Abraham Lincoln's mother, Nancy Hanks, dies.
1819	Tom Lincoln marries Sarah Johnston on December 2.
1830	Lincoln family moves to Illinois.
1831	Abraham Lincoln moves to New Salem on the Sangamon River.
1832	Abraham Lincoln joins the army to fight Chief Black Hawk.
1833	Abraham Lincoln appointed postmaster of New Salem.
1834	Lincoln elected to the Illinois legislature. He serves in the lower house for eight straight years.
1836	September 9, Lincoln passes the law exams.
1837	April 15, Lincoln moves to Springfield, Illinois. With another legislator, Dan Stone, Lincoln makes public his views against slavery.
1842	November 4, Abraham Lincoln marries Mary Todd. He continues to practice law in Illinois.
1846	Lincoln is elected to the United States House of Representatives in Washington, D.C.
1849	Lincoln returns to his successful law practice in Springfield.
1850s	The question of slavery divides the nation. Lincoln takes an open stand against the westward spread of slavery.
1856	Lincoln joins the two-year-old Republican Party.
1858	Lincoln nominated for the United States Senate by the Republicans. He runs against Stephen A. Douglas. He loses the election, but his debates with Douglas make him famous.
1860	November 6, Abraham Lincoln is elected the sixteenth President of the United States.
1861	March 4, Lincoln takes his oath of office. April 12, the Civil War starts when the South attacks Fort Sumter in South Carolina.
1862	Fighting continues between the North and the South.
1863	January 1, Abraham Lincoln signs the Emancipation Proclamation.
1863	The North wins the Battle of Gettysburg (July 1-3). President Lincoln gives his Gettysburg Address on November 19.
1864	Lincoln is re-elected. General Grant heads the Union army.
1865	April 9, General Lee surrenders to General Grant at Appomattox Courthouse. April 14, Abraham Lincoln is fatally shot by John Wilkes Booth.

About the Author:

Susan Dye Lee enjoys a varied career as historian, teacher, and writer. After studying history and English at DePauw University, she began teaching and writing professionally in 1961. Working with the Social Studies Curriculum Center at Northwestern University, she created course materials in conjunction with her teaching responsibilities. Ms. Lee has also co-authored a text on Latin America and Canada, helped develop case studies in legal history for the Law in American Society Project, and written numerous filmstrips and teacher's guides for audio-visual materials in American history. For Childrens Press, she and her husband, John R. Lee, co-authored a series of books on the American Revolution, which they completed shortly before Dr. Lee's death in 1976.

Ms. Lee's special interest is women in history. She has developed a filmstrip series on the sex roles of men and women, as well as teaching courses on the topic. Currently, she is completing her history dissertation on the Woman's Christian Temperance Union for Northwestern University.

In her free moments, Susan Lee enjoys traveling, playing the piano, and reading. During the summer, she explores northern Wisconsin from her cottage in Woodruff. A native of Cincinnati, Ohio, Ms. Lee presently makes her home in Evanston, Illinois.

About the Artist:

Ralph Canaday has been involved in all aspects of commercial art since graduation from the Art Institute of Chicago in 1959. As an illustrator, designer and sculptor his work has appeared in many national publications, textbooks, and corporate promotional material.

He is currently working on his "Famous Aviators" series, a collection of life-size bronze busts in limited edition of such aviators as the Baron Von Richthofen, Charles Lindbergh, Eddie Rickenbacker and Amelia Earhart. His knowledge of aviation history garnered through years of collecting, reading and flying have made him an "expert" in this area. He is also continually working on his aviation illustrations which are natural adjunct to his "hobby". Ralph lives in Hanover Park, Illinois with his wife Arlene, who is also in publishing.